Flying Out with the Wounded

New York University Press gratefully acknowledges the support of Madeline and Kevin Brine in making these awards possible.

■ *The New York University Press Prizes for Fiction and Poetry* ■

In 1990, New York University Press launched the Bobst Awards for Emerging Writers to support innovative, experimental, and important fiction and poetry. As the prestige of the awards has expanded in recent years, so too has their mandate. The awards were originally conceived to publish authors whose work had not yet appeared in book form. We now include authors who, while often already a known quantity, remain unrecognized relative to the quality and ambition of their writing.

We have thus renamed the awards the New York University Press Prize for Fiction and the New York University Press Prize for Poetry. In 1996, the jurors selected Jane Ransom's novel, *Bye-Bye*, and Anne Caston's collection of poems, *Flying Out with the Wounded*.

Flying Out with the Wounded

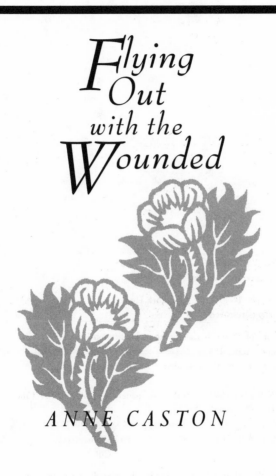

ANNE CASTON

NEW YORK UNIVERSITY PRESS
New York and London

NEW YORK UNIVERSITY PRESS
New York and London

Copyright © 1997 by New York University

Library of Congress Cataloging-in-Publication Data
Caston, Anne, 1953–
Flying out with the wounded / Anne Caston.
p.   cm.
ISBN 0-8147-1561-3 (cloth : alk. paper). — ISBN 0-8147-1560-5
(pbk. : alk. paper)
I. Title.
PS3553.A8149F58   1997   96-45903
811'.54 — dc21   CIP

New York University Press books are printed on acid-free paper,
and their binding materials are chosen for strength and durability.

Manufactured in the United States of America

10 9 8 7 6 5 4 3 2 1

CONTENTS

THE ONES WHO COME

ACKNOWLEDGMENTS

Grateful acknowledgment is made to the following publications in which these poems, or earlier versions of them, appeared:

Connections:	"Graveyard Shift"
	"Children of Holocausts"
Explorations '96:	"Flying Out with the Wounded"
	"The Burned Boy"
Free Lunch:	"Stumbling into a Pecan Grove at
	Midnight Just after the Lynching"
Maryland Poetry Review:	"Tumor"
New York Quarterly:	"Anatomy"
Permafrost:	"Lessons"
The Potomac Review:	"Graveyard Shift"
River Styx:	"Lizard Whiskey: A Parting Gift
	from Viet Nam"

My personal acknowledgment and appreciation goes also

to St. Mary's College of Maryland and the University of Wisconsin-Madison for the generous support and encouragement they have provided for me as a writer,

to the St. Mary's County Arts Council for a grant which enabled me to pursue this work,

to Hilary Tham and Bob Ayers for their insights and suggestions on this manuscript, to my teachers: Joan Aleshire, Grace Cavalieri, Lucille Clifton, Michael Glaser, Marie Howe, Pablo Medina, Thomas Sexton, and Ellen Bryant Voigt,

to Ken Flynn,

and to my husband, Ian Gallimore.

Flying Out with the Wounded

GRAVEYARD SHIFT

ANATOMY

When Hal Pingle was thirty minutes late
I walked to the long, windowed wall
along the back of the Anatomy Lab
and passed myself back and forth
through the dull midwinter afternoon light
watching how the dust motes
scattered then closed again behind.

Outside the snow had begun;
the courtyard was a muffle of voices.
In the unlit center of the room, a wheeled
gurney: a cadaver, covered with clear plastic.
Even from a distance I could make out the blue-grey
shape of the man, the dark massed areas of hair
along his upper chest and groin, the long incision
where he'd been opened at the morgue.

I didn't want the first nude man I'd see to be dead.
I didn't want to empty him out alone,
piece by piece, his entrails, his heart.
What I wanted was for my friend to arrive,
to take up the instruments and begin the excisions,
the litany of organs. I would label and bag.
Then together we'd examine the corridors leading
to and from the faulty heart, make precise notes:
where the blood pooled in his body,
what it drained away from.

                    And so not to look
at the gurney, I studied the instruments: steel calipers,
thin cannulas, the razor-bright edges of scalpels.
How sharp? I wondered even as the fat pad
of my left thumb opened and blood seeped out.

At the pale blue door labeled *Supply* in the back of the room,
I put out my good hand and turned the handle.
I heard the latch click. I heard the hinge complain.
But I was watching my thumb separate
and swell purple like a seam on a plum.
When I did look up, I was inside.
The closet lifted into long shelves
where fetuses, for as far as I could see,
swam in jars, yellowed, curled in on themselves.
The door slammed shut behind me.

I stood there in the crypt-like dark and felt — what?
Felt the silence entering my ear? Felt a corridor opening in me?
A corridor like *knowing,* or the edge of *knowing?*
Inside me, the seed of the tree of knowledge
took root and began a furious blooming.

I heard him come in. Heard him call my name.
Heard him mutter to himself; heard him leave again.
I heard a small noise that sounded like mice.
The sleeve of my labcoat was sticky. I turned in the dark.
I found the handle and opened the door.
I stepped out; I didn't look back.
I closed the blinds and locked the outer door; I turned off
all the lights but one.

Then I went to the gurney
and pulled the covering off the man. I looked
at him, at all of him. Nothing to distinguish him:
no moles, tattoos, no birthmarks or scars.
Only the incision running from sternum to pubic thicket.
I couldn't tell clearly where the wound ended
and the body began. I ran the seam of my thumb
along the long opened seam on the man.
"Here is where we meet," I told him,
"Here is where we are the same."

Casualties

1. Night Shift, V.A. Hospital

Regret plays its reedy flute in the dark
and fear blows down again from the stars
filling the trenches of men who are hunched
here in the late years of the war.
And among them is this boy
who has to be sedated now to sleep,
boy who chews the sweet root of oblivion
and fires his gun all night into the dead
who, having been delivered of their bodies,
can sin no more nor ask him again for mercy.

2. Amputee Ward

I felt the heat that rose
when I touched the swollen stump
where the leg used to be,

when I ran the light white gauze
touch of my fingers along that seam
which seeped a little in response.

I felt too the shudder that moved
through you: the unexpected pleasure
your body took against its pain.

And then you turned away from me,
embarrassed that I knew.
Beautiful, wounded boy.

3. Emergency Room: D.O.A.

What did you think your mother would do,
turning along the fence into the north pasture,
stumbling on you there: face-down in thick clover,
shot through with a bullet from her gun?

And what of your father, just then
settling with the evening news,
her screams rising to him through the screen door,
through the Georgia dusk?

And your brother, just home from the war
when the word came to him, long distance,
when that fist of *suicide* entered his ear too,
like *friendly fire*.

4. Burn Ward, St. Vincent's

All night we work over the charred
bodies of those who will not
rise from their beds and go out again.
We do little more than hold them for a time:
until the spirit lifts,
until their pain carries them
beyond us and the brackish waters.

From the brute ground of their dying
we pull ourselves into the morning air,
the sweet burnt smell of them on our clothes,
the phantoms of their bodies in our hands
needing to be whole again. We move
between the living and the dying,
heavy footed, pocked with grief.

5. *Intensive Care Unit: Coma Patient*

Only the world outside you moves.
The rest is slumber now, sleep deep as death,
where the wheel-drawn curse of your heart has fixed you,
spelled and thorny, to the trellis of your body.

Your heart hangs, a bat in its cave,
wings folded, sightless,
sending out a little sonar.

Sleeper, the map's in hand.
Already the briars fall away.

Search & Rescue: Yukon Territory, 1981

It was the boy's shoe, our third day out,
scuffed and muddied, tipped on its side,
strings still tied in a double knot
that led us up the mountain:
this way . . . this way,
in the surging rain. It took us
four days more, even with the dogs.

For those four days, his mother, dry eyed,
rocked and held to that shoe
and would not give it over.

For those four days, his father slept and woke
in a Teslin bar and cried
and tried to drink himself beyond her face.

The boy was found where someone dropped him
days before, feet first, into a shallow drain.
The rain had done the rest.

While we looked on, he was lifted out,
blue and cold. The rain had stopped.
Even the wind withheld itself.
Sun touched the trees openly;
birds sang in a nearby thicket.
Now there are whole days
I am not a part of.

Graveyard Shift

In the morgue upstairs, there are three
refrigerated drawers, set apart from the others: for dead
infants. A large body wouldn't fit.
                                        Earlier tonight,
I lifted two babies in my arms, minutes apart, washed them,
wrapped them in blue receiving blankets,
wrote down their names,
and delivered them into those cold crypts.

                                        Afterwards,
I rode the elevator down again to the floor where living
babies still pull the air hard into their lungs,
where the croup tents, like chilly amniotic sacs,
frost with breath.

                        Most nights here, the beds and cribs
are filled — twenty of them — and all night long
the two of us assigned to this shift move on rounds
from infant to infant in the dim-lit midnight nursery.
In case there's a fire or tornado, some unforeseen
catastrophe, we each have an apron with six pockets
so we can carry that many babies, plus two in arms,
down the stairwell and into the air outside.

                                        Two a.m. and two more
babies succumb. Now there are four vacant beds. Mickie says,
"Well, now we have enough pockets, don't we?"
I take the elevator up again. I tuck one baby
into his crypt. But the other has to lie
all night among grown men.

When the sun comes up,
I go home. My children want to make cookies today
so I tie on my apron, the apron with a single pocket,
and all morning we laugh and sing; we roll the ginger-brown
dough over the flour-covered table,
cut it into the shapes of boys.

We put them into the oven,
and when they are done, we take them out again,
paint icing-colored smiles on their faces.
From the counter all day, they wave and wave.

KYRIE

Each night now, God takes the horizon
in His great jaw and grinds
the edges of the seen world
into darkness and stars.

I say *God.* Perhaps
I am wrong about that part though.

If so, I blame my father for the error
who said to me of every thing, *It is God's will:* sun
rising faithfully in the east, going down in the west.
Geese lifting off each fall into skies
hung with threads of early snow.
Ruined crops. Babies born dead.

God's ways are mysterious, my father always said.

And childish, too, I think.
God plays an old game: hide-and-seek.
He hides. We seek.

> *Kyrie Eleison. Kyrie. Eleison. Kyrie . . .*

*   *   *

The God I pray to now is not
    the God of the burning bush, God
        of rams and thickets, old
            God of the *thou shalt not,* God
Alpha and Omega.

14

The God I pray to is the God
   of judas goats, God of the boats
      pushed out to sea at night, God
         of the lost-minded and stammering, old
deaf-mute, doddering God.

     *   *   *

Even where love has run to ruin,
even under the ice-heavy eaves of winter,
at the thin gullies where deer no longer come to drink,
and to the musty murmurs between the walls of my house,
I have stood and listened, certain that somewhere God was
    moving.

Others too have leaned on an elbow upright in the night,
a wind rising, and believed it was God. But no;
only a loose board clapping against a far off wall.
And in the morning, the same bright sun, the same
hunger in the gut, and trains arriving, unloading,
    departing . . .

Why lean like this, each night, into a world
emptied out as the hollows of broken bells
or fix my eyes on the darkness between the stars
if not to search out the old God of my father,
to call Him out and make Him answer for what is happening
    here?

     *   *   *

Against the Lord of this Hour,
    against the God of this Bleak Day,
I have made myself
    blind, have made myself at last
deaf and dumb.

Still my traitorous fingers
    go on signing His name in the dark.
Cut off my hands, will you?
    Hang them at the gate.
Any gate will do.

The Burned Boy

It falls to me, the task: to lift him
by his knobbly elbows — the unburned parts of him —
to dip him slowly into the whirlpool and float the charred
    skin off.
So twice each night I lift him and twice each night he screams
through the lifting and lowering and the lifting out again.

I'd like to say he sings his pain.
It isn't singing though and not even for my sake, or yours, or
    his,
can I make anything else of the boy's convulsing
or the stench of scorched skin and underskin
that rises from the water's surface, catches in my throat, and
    gags me.

It goes like this between us, the ritual movement
in and out of pain and revulsion, the terrible cryings-out,
until one night he opens his mouth,
neck muscles bulging with the effort,
but no sound comes, only the stirring of waters
and the retching I can't hold back.

In my dreams of the burned boy, I'm setting rosebushes in
among beds of blue forget-me-nots and baby's breath.
When I look over, he's propped among the thorned,
stubbly bushes: mute, gnarled elbows out.
He makes no sound as I lift him, as I ease him
into a sun-warmed puddle of mud and clay,
set him in, give him water, wait for him to bloom.

17

FLYING OUT WITH THE WOUNDED

When the lightning struck, trees blackened against
a silver sky and the river bruised, the undersides of clouds
wounding its surface. But this was not my work. My work,
pressed into the dark hold of the chopper, was a drunk
man—foul and fuming, restrained against his drunkenness,
his abdomen packed with gauze to staunch the bleeding—and
his head-on victims: a woman and a girl whose head had been
bandaged to keep the brain intact.
The girl was dead.

We lifted off with our cargo. There
were scant inches in which to crouch. Jack had to ride in
front. I was airsick and praying that the snarl of blades
overhead wouldn't snag in the electric night.

Somewhere
between that stretch of sky and Birmingham, the man caught
sight of the woman and girl. "Goddamn," he said, "Goddamn.
Gooks." And then, to me, "In 'Nam we used to throw 'em
out, watch 'em splatter." He laughed and laughed to himself.
The woman flinched. She turned her face from him, went
back to stroking the girl's cheek. The girl's gaze was fixed.
Still the woman was making the shushing sound. I leaned
over the man. "Shut up," I said close to his ear so he would
hear me over the noisy blades; "Shut up or I will push *you*
out." He quieted then and I sat back to ride the airsickness in
me out.

Can I tell you I liked thinking about pushing him

out? Can I say I was imagining how easy it would be for me to roll the man out into the rumble of thunder and the whirring blades? I was.

But then he seized. He arched against his bonds. His eyes rolled back to white. I straddled the man; I called out for help. Jack grabbed the ambu bag and started the count. I placed my hands, palms down, against that spot two fingers' breadth from the tip of the sternum. I pushed: the man's wound gushed, wet and warm, against my thighs. The smell of blood thickened. I wanted to lift myself from him. Still I pushed the man's heart to respond. Still Jack counted. Still the ambu bag wheezed in and out.

We worked like that the whole way in, and when we landed someone else took over. They lifted him away; I stepped out to catch a mouthful of wet, clean air, to drive the blood-drunk smell of him from my lungs. I looked down then and saw myself: bloodied, where I had straddled the man, as if I had just given birth.

My Patient Jumps to His Death

I don't know; there were signs, there are
　　always signs. Like the crucifix he handed me,
　　　　how he rubbed the stump where his leg
　　　　　　used to be and shrugged, "I've given up on God."

Maybe the way I imagine it now isn't the way it was,
　　but a newspaper photograph is what I have of the event:
　　　　him, mid-air, the first sun catching the gold in his hair,
　　　　　　and the white sheet he'd wrapped himself in

fluttering loose in the wind his falling made.
　　Someone who'd been on the ground told me
　　　　it had come to rest at the tips of his fingers
　　　　　　like a white flag of *truce* or *surrender.*

Or maybe it was just a sheet.
　　The tendency is to make something meaningful
　　　　of whatever doesn't make sense.
　　　　　　I do it myself.

Looking at this photograph, his body
　　the only bright thing against the dark
　　　　face of the building and the predawn sky,
　　　　　　I swear what goes through my head

is: *Lucifer, falling from heaven.*

Maybe the earth is a mirror of heaven.

Maybe heaven did tremble, did go briefly

dark and still just after Lucifer fell.

And maybe the seraphim folded their six wings

over their faces and the cherubims' *Hosannahs* stalled.

Maybe eternity was washed, after that, in a ruined light.

And maybe somewhere at the farthest edge,

at the seam called *Mercy* where heaven meets hell,

maybe the Angel of Purgatory was pushing a cart,

carrying a cup of water, when she entered his room,

saw the empty bed, the open window,

the white curtains fluttering there like the sleeves of saints.

WARMING THE BLOOD

When the bleeder's brought in
just after midnight, he's cool to the touch,
like a dead man already, he's lost
so much blood and we're losing him.

It isn't blood; we've got plenty of that,
typed and crossmatched before he arrived.
But it's refrigerated, all of it, cold,
and the one working warmer is slow.

So we fill a pan with hot water
and float a bag: two minutes,
beginning to end. Not fast enough.
He's shivering.

Because he's cold, or because he's dying,
I turn and push an icy bag
into the warm darkness under my clothes—
my breasts, my stomach, my sides,

my underarms warming the blood,
three, four, five units at a time
until I'm shivering,
until I'm in it with him,

caught up in the chill of *death:*
the skin a winter pond and, in the deep
underrooms and chambers of the body,
the blood slowing to a last red frieze.

The Last Lobotomized Woman

I can't say it frightens me, the fury I feel at each night's end,
   the stern and sudden aftermath of triage

passing through the body, the heart; and it isn't
   the midnight pain and longing of the wounded

from which I have to haul myself each morning
   when my shift is done.

What frightens me is how, in order to be with you like this
   in the daylight world, I have to put that other world aside,

and the devastation that comes with knowing and denying
   it is there, always, just underneath the bright-lit world

in which we walk and have our lives.
   And, more than that, it frightens me

that a void yawns and stretches and opens itself in me then,
   like the emptiness in the body just after giving birth,

that stillness where something moved before,
   where something had raged

and kicked itself free of the slick darkness.
   After making love to my husband this morning, I catch

a glimpse of myself in the beveled mirror over the dresser,
   my body done rocking through the motions of loving.

An emptiness has been in me now for years.
   But I look so ordinary: a woman

tangled in bedsheets, disheveled and flushed,
   a dim smile settling into place again

while he showers and dresses for work. I look at my face
   and think of her, the last lobotomized woman:

how still she always sat; how well behaved and quiet
   she was, even among the insane,

half-sunk in the shadows of the asylum dayroom.
   She was the only still point in that room:

tables overturned, books knocked to the floor,
   punches and shouts and, always, the television:

that chaos of black and white,
   gray voices from a high corner of the room.

In a scuffle once, someone threw a checkerboard
   and she was hit: her head slammed over to one side,

her glasses shattered on the floor.
   But she sat perfectly still,

a little crooked in her chair.
   One of the crazies went over to her;

he yelled in her face, *I'm sorry!* — as if she were hard of hearing.
   When she didn't respond, he shrugged; he took her face

in his hands and tilted her head upright again. That half-smile
   was still on her face; her hands were folded in her lap.

She went on looking beyond him.
    He sat down at her feet. *Poor thing,*

he said, and then to us: *the poor dear thing.*
    The room grew still;

the television flickered and rolled.
    The man at her feet began to cry.

Poor thing, he said, over and over,
    and the dayroom crazies sank finally

under the weight of such pity;
    they all began to cry.

For no reason I can make sense of now,
    except perhaps just that they wept,

something in her face flickered and she seemed to see them.
    She lifted one hand to the man at her knee,

as if she would touch his face.
    She seemed deeply troubled.

I remember seeing . . . , she said to him,
    I remember seeing . . . I remember . . .

Then whatever it was
    was gone. Her hands fell to her lap again,

the vacant smile descended.
    The dull door of her face closed.

Hands

Surgery last night on a man slight as a boy,
his chest unbuttoned, flapped open like a shirt;
his heart fell to strings in my hands.
They put it back and sewed him up again.

Whose work do I do—half
sister to God, half sister to Mengele—hunched each night
with a cup of water, with bandages, with morphine
to ease the dying from crumbling bodies into the afterlife?

My hands on hot brows, on pulses, on pain,
I rustle bed to bed, in the half-light
half-dark of makeshift wards,
Der Weiße Engel,

and I carry home on my white hands at dawn
the thick ether smell of death,
a phantom that rises in bright morning rooms
each time I pull a brush through my hair.

Washing up this morning, I can't
bring my hands to my face. Such hands:
a man's heart falls apart.

MERCY

Pediatric Oncology, Mercy Memorial Hospital

1.

Oh, as for mercy, I can tell you—I
who, for years, have hauled the corpses from littered
roads and hillsides to cool, indifferent morgues—I can tell
    you
there is little left of mercy in this world, God's or otherwise.

What there is today
is a cracked blue cup on the windowsill
that holds water scarcely well enough
to keep a boy's fistful of buttercups standing.

And there is this boy.

Otherwise, it would be just like the cynic I am
to pitch the yellow weeds and the busted cup.
But then he would wake, you see, his eyes
flitting to that sill, and it would be empty, as the bed

was empty next to him when the other boy died in the night.
His eyes would be full again of that terrible knowing . . .
Still, how merciful can it be to let a sick boy think
for even one more day that a cup of water is sufficient

to keep any mortal thing alive?

2.

We went downstairs at midnight to tell
his weary parents: that it was
a good passing, that he did not suffer, that he went
to sleep and, after a minute, just stopped breathing.
His father fell back hard in his chair as a man does
who has been given a strong blow to the jaw.
But his mother: she blinked and looked up at us
as if she didn't understand; she asked in a quiet voice,
Do you mean he's dead?

Dead. Yes. A difficult word to say
straight up—the way she said it—
when the dead one is a child. She screamed then,
a long scream. And another. And another. And none of us
could comfort her and nothing we did could stop her.
Neither could we bring the boy back.
Down the dark street, a factory siren
let out a long blast. An ambulance
answered below.

3.

A boy dying in the night in this city
is not a new story. Many children die here.
And in great pain. That he did not go in pain
might console you.

Does it?

HEARTWOOD

In time, a bridge, and on it a woman
who waits to usher the dying into eternity:
Modgudr, Morg-ana, An-gurboda,
Mother of Hel.
I have been that woman.

Over the river Wailing,
over its dark water-song
I have watched the living world
go bright, have watched it cry itself
into the light again after the dead have crossed.

And I have watched those
who are crossing over into death,
how they spend what hours are left
forgiving the things that held them,
forgiving the things that let them go.

And now, from the rough-hewn, splintered
heart of the oak, I fashion an oar
with which to row myself away.
And while I row, I sing,
with my whole heart, rowing and singing

until only the stars are left to listen in,
the solid, grainy heart of oak
rising and falling, rising and falling,
moving me home again
through the sweet black waters.

LESSONS

When I Am Not Telling It

Somewhere in history a woman
is tying on her apron just at the moment
the rough hemp rope is knotted
fast around her husband's neck.

The snap as it takes
the man's full weight,
and the brief inelegant steps
of his feet in midair —

this is someone else's story.

And the child with gallows-dreams,
the woman's child, who would be my great-grandfather
waking the household nightly crying,
Papa, oh my Papa —

this too is someone else's story.

But this silence which is the long silence of my life
out of which the story rises when it rises
and to which the story returns
when I am not telling it,

this is my story

as is the old knock and shove of my heart around it
and my love of grudges.

To begin with an apron and end
with a hanging, crying between:
this is a story I know
well enough to tell.

THE BURNING

If you can't say something nice, don't say anything at all.

1.

From one end of my childhood
to the other, the silence of obedience
stretches, lifts and curls
like wisps of smoke around me.

Where there's smoke, there's fire, they say.
And the furnace in me is rage.

Now every chair I sit in, every pew,
each table or book or photograph I put my hands on
smoulders. Every thing I love goes up in flames.
I am the torch put to it.

Some things are better left unsaid.
I understand: a mantle of normalcy over things.
Good girl. Good wife. Good mother.

2.

Listen. The medusa is an obvious ruse:
the head of snakes, the stone-gray eyes, the scaly
body of a beast. You know to bring along a shield,
some mirror by which to save yourself.

You think you're safe?
Just put your hands on me. That warmth you feel
will change to burning. Incendiary. That's my heart.
And all the heat moves out from there.

3.

As a girl, I got so good at smouldering
not even my petticoats were singed.
My hair lay down in perfect waves around me.
My shoes were patent, black
reflections of the rooms I entered; my face genteel.

Only my voice was charred,
riddled with smoke, but who knew that?
I rarely spoke. *Yes ma'am. Yes sir.*
That hardly qualifies as speech.

4.

For me, it is always eight minutes before
or eight minutes after, the warmth or the chill,
never the event itself.

Or maybe the eighth minute before
is the sun gone dark
and the next seven minutes
already *afterlife.*

I was four.
A girl in my mother's house.
The man was not my father.

5.

I am burning still; with shame,
with more than shame.

Over twenty-one million
minutes beyond it, and though I can't see his face,
I can feel that arm, the one he later lost, the right arm—
arm that he held me with so his left hand could grope below.

And my mother, woman in the mirror,
eight minutes after, as the ruin set in,
what did she see; what did she
look away from?

MY FATHER'S HOUSE

There are no roads back to that house:
55 Odessa Drive, our backyard
separated from the wild field by a hedge,

where each morning, I lifted into the low blue sky
on a plank swing and I sang
the nonsense rhymes and syllables

only a six-year-old can get away with:
mumbo-jumbo, eat your gumbo,
Peter-beater, booger-eater . . .

How little else I can remember now:
the hot kitchen where my grandmother cooked and sewed,
cornbread crumbled into buttermilk at noon,

orange marigolds lifting along the gravel drive.
I remember it was the first house
death visited: the pink-white froth

on the dog's black mouth
as he staggered through the hedge and across the yard
where my brother and I were digging for worms.

I remember my grandmother
running from the porch, her dress hiked up
over her bony knees, the way she placed herself

between us and the dog,
the raggedy broom she shook at him.
Stay back, she said to us, *he's mad—he's got the rabies.*

I can't remember now which neighbor called
the dog catcher who came and netted the dog
and put him down with a long needle on our front lawn.

But I do remember how, for the rest of that afternoon,
I swung in the dangerous yard and tried
the new words, *mad* and *rabies,* on my tongue.

Singing, always singing, no matter what—and dunking.
Singing and dunking. Though drinking's not allowed. Nor
    dancing.
Too close to fornication; too *Methodist*. But singing and dunking
Baptists are well-acquainted with, even the youngest,
though dunking can seem a lot like drowning at eight years old

if you step off into those cold waters, starting to sink,
and the preacher slaps a white cloth over your nose and
    mouth
and spills you over backwards and you lose your footing
and your good manners as unexpectedly as you lost your
    heart to Jesus
that April morning when the congregation was singing the
    Easter sun home.

Going under, all sinner again and desperate for solid ground,
I clawed the preacher's arms and face,
until he had to stand me up again, fast; he shook me hard
    then, twice,
and my teeth clacked against each other from more than the
    chilly
waters and the fear of drowning, while the choir in front of us,

oblivious, sang again the old refrain:
Almost persuaded, now to believe . . .

First Rebellion, 1959

By mid-December, we all were weary of the chronic
colds and ringworm we'd gotten from crouching
in the far wet winter ditches of the schoolyard
once, sometimes twice, a week
when the civil defense sirens sounded.
But there was Castro to consider, in a country called Cuba
which, we all knew, was far away from Florida but not far
    enough.

So between rehearsing the *Adeste Fideles* and *Stille Nacht*
for parents' night at Christmas, the sirens blared
and we found ourselves, again, shin-deep
in the muddy waters of the irrigation ditch
that ran between the schoolyard and the cane fields.

The principal walked up and down with his megaphone
and pointed at the ones who tried to stay half-standing,
Get down. Get down, I say. If the missiles fall. . .

Lucy Armstrong, next to me, began to cry—she always cried
at the part about the missiles falling on us.
Then Charlene Baxter was crying. And I started crying too.
Not because of the missiles, but because I'd crouched
so low my new underpants were wet and because something
moved by me underwater and I was afraid
it was the baby cottonmouths
which, as everyone knew, swam in ditchwater and had bad

tempers and could kill you with one drop of their poison.
Soon the whole class was crying.

Miss Holtz, who was our teacher, climbed out of the ditch
and said something to the principal we couldn't hear.
Her legs had brown ditch-muck on them and the back
seams of her stockings were crooked.
She called us into two-by-two lines and marched us
back into the classroom, even though the all-clear hadn't
    sounded.

We took to our seats in our soggy clothes.
We folded our hands and waited.

Miss Holtz, who was the only Jew we knew personally
in Jacksonville which, in those days, was mostly
full of Baptists and heathens,
smoothed her wet wool skirt and emptied
the ditch water from her high black heels. She said
to us, *If Mr. Castro sends his missiles to America,*
ladies and gentlemen, we will not be cowering in ditches.
We will be here, sitting, upright in our seats.
And she took up the yellow chalk.

The Book

On a give-away table at the library when I was twelve:
gold-embossed letters on a black cloth cover.
I took it to the librarian who drew a line of little *xxxs*
through the library name and stamped
"This book belongs to_____" in the front cover.
She watched as I penciled my name in the space.
She initialed it and handed it back to me.
So it came to be my book.

*　　*　　*

When I asked my father later if it was true,
what the book said, he told me, *Girl, you can't
believe everything you read in books,*
and he went back to work on his model planes.

So I asked my teacher about it too.
She said, *Well, yes, it's true,
for the most part. It was terrible
but, after all, they killed Christ, the Jews.*

*　　*　　*

So I hid the book. I put it in a drawer, under my socks,
and late at night while the household slept, I crept out of bed
and sat at the moonlit window and turned the pages.

I let myself look at their faces,
their bony arms and legs, the barns of hair,
the little scoops of gold waiting on scales.

One page I returned to every night:
a girl who could've been my age walking, head down,
by a woman's side, carrying a book under her arm.

Just ahead of them, to the side of the gate
they will pass through: a pile,
already burning.

Stumbling into a Pecan Grove at Midnight Just after the Lynching

We'd come — the six of us — to kindle
a fire and tell our ghost stories late at night,
seeking out some dark place farthest removed
from what we knew to be the lit, sane world.
Oh hell, complained Dickie, walking in, *there's no moon;*
it won't be scary enough.

Still, the place felt like every dark
closet I ever hid in: the same soured
dirt smell of old shoes, a damp
sponge pressing the spine from behind
where mildew has rotted wallboard soft.
There were lights and voices. Far off. Moving away.

God, what's that smell? somebody asked
just about the time someone else
brushed against the body, hanging from a low limb,
and set it swinging, in the dark, like a large piñata
over us. Jake pulled out his cigarette lighter and sent up
a little flash of light. We saw him then: *the hanged man.*

He'd been lynched and set afire.
Skin hung from his arms in raw singed flags.
One shoe had fallen off, the flesh of his left foot still inside.
And as for his face, well, my nightmares are made of that.
When Dickie stopped throwing up and when our legs
could hold us again, we went to town for help.

They cut him down and laid him out like that
in the Zion Methodist Church. No one ever claimed
the body, far as I know. We learned early not to speak of it,
not even among ourselves. Dickie went north to Canada
and Jake went to Viet Nam. And as for me, I keep trying
to imagine a pecan tree—any tree really—
free of that hanged man's ghost.

BLOODLINE

For my grandfather

Dim light and warmth and the wet
feathered undersides of the hens; also how,
when I drew my gathering hand back again,
it was dappled with the blood and membrane
that slicked the morning's eggs. I remember this now
and the grizzled old man who never lifted a hand to me
though there was reason to flinch if he lashed out
to crush a fly or sever a blacksnake's head.

Once, while my brother and I looked on,
he grabbed his rifle from the truck and shot a puppy
he'd backed over — the wrong pup: and when he found
the other, wounded one which had dragged itself,
whimpering and limp, into a nearby scrub, he shot it too,
the spent cartridges clattering, one then another,
in the dirt-packed yard.

He was hard in a practical way: calves were fattened
then butchered; lambs too, even the goat.
And if he let the pig dangle by its hind feet, squealing,
while he withheld the knife all morning from its throat,
or if he laughed when the slaughtered chicken, headless,
chased us around the yard, well, some of the meanness
that ticked in him has ticked in me too.

These late years in the crowded tents of the wounded
and dying—so much blood, so many dead—and haven't I,
on bitter mornings, felt my stiff fingers thawing
in the left-over warmth of some corpse's belly?
Haven't I plunged my hands into the viscera of men's bodies
and pulled them, sticky, back to me, and felt the curious
pleasure rise in me again that rose those early mornings
when I was a child gathering eggs?

In the Tub Tonight, My Son

In the tub tonight, my son
and his favorite boats.

Go down, he says like God.
Like God, he plants one finger on each bow.
The boats oblige.

But when he lifts his hands,
the foolish things bob up again,
white-sailed and arrogant.

This angers him, the boy,
and, in a rage I have not seen in him before,
he tears the sail from each blue boat
and rends them, masts and decks and hulls.
But still, the pieces float.

He rises then,
the water on his small boy's body
shimmering; he pulls the plug.

Go down, he says once more.

They do, for good: blue shards
scattered, beached around his feet
on the sandy, white bottom of the tub.

He stands, a stranger to me almost,
amid the devastation he has wrought,
then seems, a moment, lost; he shivers
and steps from the tub.

Late into the night, I hear
him in the dark house
crying for his beautiful boats.

At Passover

The night before the kosher butcher is due,
    half in, half out of dreams, I wait for my children to sleep,
        for my husband's snores to knock against the dark
            walls of the clapboard house.

And while I wait, I finger the sky-blue lambswool
    shawl I pulled last winter. I wrap myself in it,
        and when the household sleeps, I slip out to the far
            pasture where the ewes and their lambs are penned.

Perhaps *only* because of that shawl
    they let me pass, the wild-eyed mothers
        who have rushed at us for days as if they knew
            the season of slaughter was on them again.

Only a perfect male will be taken,
    so I have only one to mar.
        In my left hand, a tendril of ivy;
            in my right hand, a kitchen knife.

He finds me right away, the black
    beads of his eyes button-bright;
        he wobbles over to
            nuzzle my hand for the ritual

treat he is used to; he sinks
    his muzzle deep into the pale wool
        comfort of the shawl. *Now,* I tell myself,
            cut now; one flaw and he will be spared . . .

But in the end, I cannot do it,
    not even to save his life;
        we are locked together in the blessing
            and the curse of his perfection.

So I lift him into my soft-shawled arms.
    I murmur and hold to him while,
        over our heads, the stars wink out one by one.
            I ask him to forgive me, as if that were possible.

When they separate him out next morning,
    the pasture erupts with bleating; but he goes,
        willing and dumb, nuzzling the butcher's hand
            while a blessing is sung over him.

SUICIDE NOTES

When I return from the shore
dogwoods are snowing out on the lawn
and your message is on my machine.

*   *   *

You have always been in such a hurry
to drop yourself into hell
and this time I can't pull you back.

*   *   *

I'm afraid to look at you there
deep in your coma, afraid in that one bare look
the ragged rigging of my own life will fail to hold.

*   *   *

Never again will I be so far away
while you are at home
dressing yourself for the funeral.

*   *   *

Never again will you die like this:
the diastolic night dropping out from under you,
the clock's face turning,

blue forget-me-nots crowding your throat.

AfterLife

For my father

1.

I stumbled on him,
aisle five, between the pasta and the breads,
where he was wandering up and down
the long deserted aisle alone. He was
two, maybe three, years old,
in jeans and a bright red jacket.

So I stalled,
feigned interest in the rye and sourdough,
and waited for some frantic mother to return.
He sat down — lay down really — on a vacant shelf
and I thought, *She'll never see him there.*

"Where's
your mother?" I asked and he began to cry,
as if he'd just remembered her. Shoppers passed over us
like so much produce they weren't interested in.

By the time
Social Services arrived, he was sleeping, one fist curled
against his chin. As they left the aisle with him
he opened his eyes and cried out for me.

So I carried the boy
as far as the curb, his hands tangled in my hair;
when I handed him over, he cried. I smiled.
I waved *goodbye*. I said they'd find
his mother for him.

53

As if he understood.

     It was the last I saw of him
and, like some photograph, his face is burned
behind my brain: *the lost boy.*

   2.

       Father, how can I believe
that the soul lifts off at death, turning forever
from the body? How can I believe that tonight
when even the rain, the prodigal rain, returns
to the dust-crazed windows and something in it
brings the boy's face back to me again?
       And too there is the wind,
rain's old companion, straining at the gate's hasp,
its raspy comings and goings. All those
settings-off and it too returns, finally,
fingering the things it has loved
even if they have fallen, all,
in the meantime, to rust.
      Father, if there is a heaven
to run to after death, let it be free of the boy's face,
looking back at me. If not, then let me be
here, in my one dark life, as I am tonight:

         letting go

the angels, the grim God, all the bright glories
of whatever else moves over the face of the deep,
the soul here-and-now in the blood-thick body,
a damp thing, a dark wind, some memory of a lost boy's face:

that noisy shadow clinging at the heels, the elbows,
to the body's firm, familiar earth.

               So, Father, tell me:
what is the dark to you?

To the Woman in the Next Bed
Whose Daughter Was Born with Down's Syndrome
the Day My Daughter Was Born Dead

I can't remember your name anymore,
but all these years and I am trying still
to forget your face when they first handed her to you
bundled into a pale pink blanket, the devastation
that shattered your sea-blue eyes
when you saw what the doctor had spoken was true.

Years later, and it comes back to me clear: your wrecked face
over the nursing child and how my bound breasts let go
with each suck and slurp that reached me there
through the white curtain the nurse had drawn between us.
When the child had been lifted from you again and the gauze
barrier pushed back, I envied you your sweet, retarded girl.

We didn't speak then; instead we let the television
drone on for hours, let it flicker and fall, at last,
to a midnight silence, let it go dark and leave the two of us
awkward in the hush of that room.
Your voice, pitched thin and high, broke the silence then:
Do you think it's right for me to still name her Hope?

Because you shoved your fist against your mouth and wept,
and bitterly, I bit back the cruel thing I would have said to you:
that this is the face Hope wears in this world,
the idiot's face, sweet and keen with hunger,
swaddled and handed over, a living thing,
to only the fortunate ones.

Waiting Room

1. My Husband Sends Flowers

Not like this
will I be pacified.

Was it, as his card implied, some *act*
of a merciful God that never allowed
the child one mouthful of air
before being lifted away, blue and unnamed?

Who made this baby wrong?
Who made the others right?

I had thought Death would enter my house
with its meat-red breath,
with its cold blue eye fixed on me.
But Death held its blade over the child.

I walk from room to room at night
blood-heavy still from pregnancy,
grief braided into my hair,
his flowers blooming wildly on the sill.

2. The Child's Death

The day she broke from me in birth,
still for a moment sweetly strung to me,
she wore the darkness in me out and I believed in mercy.
Old Indian-giver God, I am learning sorrow now by rote.
She left much as she first arrived —
breathless, still — and I, struck so, could scarcely bear
to pick her up as now I cannot wholly lay her down.
She went from me to Death,
that garment with no seam or rift,
and my arms could not lift her out of it or take her back
or move her down the hall to bed, her small head bobbing
on my shoulder like a boat at sea.

3. I Am Asked to Play Mary in the Living Christmas Pageant

The holiday grows terrible:
the dead child's face swimming back
through tinsel and tree lights.

I would refuse it if I could:
and the midnight bells, snow falling,
the bright blood berries of the holly.
Even the crèche with its tiny infant.

But the night would break over me all the same.

So I take my place among the beasts
and the burden of gifts, waiting again
for the child to arrive,
for the child to be lifted away.

Last Lullaby for the Dead Child

The hoar-frost enters me as it enters the world outside,
crown-first, and I am going wintery as well,
even the one brief memory I have of you, slight
and blanketed in my arms, gone white or silver
where your face used to be.

Oblivion has pulled the shades.
Goodnight, my daughter; off to sleep.

It isn't dreaming that I do; a dream
would have to start somewhere—some face,
some graceless features, small but like my own, swimming up
from memory. Nothing today but the cold.
My own reflection isn't me.

LESSONS

For Matthew

I sit outside in the shade with my son,
a brown-eyed boy who clutches a baseball mitt
and perches at the edge of the front porch steps.
His hair is combed wetly, slicked out of his face;
from time to time, he spits into his hands
and smoothes his cowlick back again,
the way his father likes it.

For a time I try to comfort him
with the old lies: *Maybe the traffic got bad. Maybe*
we got the wrong time. The wrong day. I'm sure
he'll be here soon. But the boy is learning . . .

As the sun drops, the crisscrossed
wires of telephone and utility
stand out against the blazing sky
and I think of my brother who used to sit
next to me on a porch like this, silent and stunned
after my father had taught him . . . *because I love you,*
the welts on my brother's legs rising.

The sun is out now; lightning bugs are lifting on the lawn.
The boy sags against me, making two fists
and rubbing them against his eyes while I hum
and pretend, for his sake, not to notice.

Finally he sits up again, quiet and rigid,
turned away from me, his back
straight and taut as a bowstring, his silence
the arrow aimed at my heart.

Since You Asked

1.

Marriages? Oh, yes, I see. We're going to get
into that one, are we? Okay. I'll say it straight up: *five.*
I've had five marriages. Four husbands. Figure it out
for yourself. It's way beyond me.

You think you know a man. And then
you live with him a year or two. Or seven.
Have a child with him, or two, or three, or four.

You look up from your ironing one day,
see him leaning in an open doorway.
He's framed in light, his mouth working;
he's trying to tell you something,
and what you know just then
is what you don't know.

Soon he's leaving—or you are—and you're alone again
inside your grief. Or anger. Or relief. Swearing
you won't do that again.

Live in sin next time, you think.

Then some starlit evening, sunbright morning,
you blink and there you are again:
I do. I will. 'Til death . . .

2.

But not the socks and underwear; not this time.
Let them lie forever by the bedside where they've fallen;
let them rot, the stench fill up the house.
Let the hamper bulge all weekend,
with his dingy shirts, my stockings.
Let his mother whisper it's a shame
how slovenly the household looks.
Let dishes congregate at midnight in the sink,
a mass of peas and carrots drowning in cold suds.
Let the kitchen dim with fires, singed chickens, fallen cakes.

Let the sparrows gather at the windows
begging crumbs and let the neighbors wonder why
the summer grass is high enough to lose small children in.
Let the fields fall fallow; let the garden bruise with thistle.
And let the years roll, rightly, wrongly, into one another
while the gossips rage around us
Isn't she awfully older than he? Let them wonder.
And let us fall each night into our marriage bed,
answering again and again
that tangled old riddle of love and lust.

HUNGER

For Ian

On the night of our first anniversary,
while you sleep at home five hundred miles north,
the old nightmare rouses me and, doused with sweat,
I search the grassy field beyond this window
gone silver-gray by the full moon's light.
No soldiers move tonight from the wood's edge
as they moved once: a crude rumble of swearing
and boots over the broken bricks and rubble
of an abandoned mill where I crouched, and my children,
with other women and children, homeless,
on the second floor, barricaded in for the night.

They shouted up at us, those drunk soldiers,
—some of them young as I was then—
Want to earn some money, darlings?
Come down. Or let us in. We'll pay for love.
I rocked the teething baby
and covered my daughter's ears and I burned—
Lord, how I burned—to hear the flagrant
propositions they offered loudly up to us
when the whiskey'd properly fired them.

Not love, but hunger. How it drives us all,
and wrongly sometimes. I tell you, hunger is what drove me
to the first man I married, what drove me, when he'd gone,
to the streets, to actual hunger deep in the gut,

to the hand-me-down coats, to the sandwiches
and grape Koolaid the good nuns brought up to us
twice each day; it's what drove me, finally, to that mill,
to the dank night corners of the homeless and the winter
sickness which took the weakest children off,
and some of us too, to the burial carts and the charity graves.

And hunger is what will carry me back again tomorrow
to you, what carries me back, always, to the dark
embrace of this world and our difficult children,
three of them soldiers now themselves.

Maybe it's what brought those boys long ago,
in their camouflage and boots, to that mill
where we huddled: some fierce,
inexplicable hunger that drove them
to stand below, shivering in the brittle dark, calling out
what they would do for us, for our daughters,
if only we would open up to them.

And, if I thought you could stand hearing it,
I would tell you now how I considered it.
Going down, I mean. To him.
To that one, strange man in the dark who called out my name
and promised only what he would actually give and nothing
    more.

—*June 30, 1996*

KEEPING WATCH

1. The X-Rays Come Back

So, Death, this is the work
you've been about for months,
you and your Cancer chisel:
this bone shot through with light,
this hive where the bees of pain toil all day.

2. *The Body Politic*

Before the surgeon's work begins,
before the scalpel lifts part of me away,
before the gurney rolls me into recovery
and the anaesthesia mists lift,

I wait in this body riddled with the news
of distant terrors of the day:
the coups, the camps, the refugees,
the famished children, the soldiers poised . . .

O small echo of this world,
my body, tell me:
what darkness are we
falling through and into what bloody hand?

3. Filling Out the Donor Card

If I rise to go out
from the blood-cave of my body,
what would be left to someone else
and what should go out with me?

To whom could I leave these ears,
compromised and heavy,
burdened with secrets,

or these arms and legs,
these breasts, this womb that grew
accustomed to ruin?

To whom would I leave this heart
which has learned to bear
the small destructions of love?

And to whom, these eyes,
these two old witness stones—
who could bear to see again
the glory in us go down?

4. Tumor

I dream it is a small child growing in me.
He has fallen out of the moon,
a tiny angel, a pink flesh doll.
He holds out his hands to me and cries
Mama   Mama
and when I can bear it no longer,
I give him a name and go under the knife.

5. *Keeping Watch*

What I thought I saw that night was a man
rowing his longboat across a moonlit river.
He put in among the rushes
at the water's edge and stood there
as if waiting for someone.

After a while, he picked up his oar
and set off again in the dark.

He rowed directly into the path of the moon.
He was the only one in the boat.
I watched until he disappeared
into the dark at the opposite shore.
He was so much closer than I thought.

6. *Coming Home*

The sky has held.
Small stones still litter the yard.
The door opens and every thing is as when I left:
grey mice scurrying in the pantry,
a cracked blue cup on the sill,
white sheets turned back for sleep.

I enter into life again; I take it up
with all its absences.

And on everything I touch now:
the old stain of death,
or perhaps only some memory of it
which I unpack again and again
and settle into like a home.

7. *Passing the Five-Year Mark*

We have made our way through the Christmas storm,
over the reluctant ice of the river,
bearing the gifts we have learned to bear:
our survivors' bodies and the names of those we lost.
The mantle is deep in holly,
a small tree shines in its lights,
and far off in the night there are carolers
singing a song we listened to in that other season,
season of dying, when we leaned from a hospital window
and wept when we heard it and thought we would die
without knowing the world again whole.

GOD'S HEAD

Nights now, when God puts His head
    next to my head on the pillow,
        I know I'll wake next morning

with singed hair and my bald scalp glowing;
    the cuckoo will have nested in my brain
        and oblivion will have come and gone

again, leaving its dim drum in my ear. I'm waiting
    for Him anyway, though the wind rebukes me sternly
        for my sleeplessness.

Already, the whole dark vault of my body is shining
    like steel and, somewhere across the night, God
        is the Whetstone, singing for its blade.

THE ONES WHO COME

BELLS

Beyond this sun-drenched morning,
beyond the mock-blue skies and the bleating goats,

beyond the clenched fists of magnolia blooms,
beyond the bean plants, staked and upright,

and the straw-hearted scarecrow,
beyond the snap of sheets

whitening on the wire and the cat's arched back,
beyond this slight and ordinary life

the relentless bells ring and ring.

On the Subject of the Poor in America

For Robin H.

Ah, poverty. It's difficult, you see,
for me to speak about it—even to you
who would understand, or would try to—the shame
of having been that poor. Yes, shame; that old dog at the
    heels.

And what, do you imagine, would you feel:
four children—one a baby still—a husband gone,
house taken, and the last bottle of milk
gone sour. You'd feel responsible.
And failed. And then there'd be that baby, his eyes
on you, fever-bright. Always that baby
who doesn't cry, who doesn't blame you, ever.

Even clothed and fed as I am now, content
in middle-America, I can tell you: poverty is
the only country I've ever really known,
its bleak and populated terrain.
I know its faces, its filthy
fingers in my pockets.
Its tattered flag flies over my dreams.

But let me tell you, comfort is an old devil too,
minus horns and pitchfork, true,
but a devil nevertheless. In the ear
day and night, his smooth, convincing voice:
Try not to think of them, those others. You got out;

they could too if they wanted to. Just have your life.
Be grateful for warm bread, cool waters, the safe
walls of a house, the view. This is where you belong . . .

But the poor are always refugees, and so are we, my friend,
so are we. Refugees with no boats, no roads away
from what we know. No ports of liberty to sail to.
Not for us. And not for those
who know the turning worm of hunger in the gut.

Say we do get something finally — comfort
or love, four solid walls around us, heat,
a sapling in the yard, a baby who thrives —
it's never going to be enough
and it's always going to be too much.

As long as we know
they're there, those others — and we do,
God knows we do — there's guilt for us in every mouthful.
The biscuit goes down, difficult; the crumbs
impossible to leave.

After the Siege

1.

I am thinking tonight of those children,
how easily they slipped from us.

The wings of sorrow open in me,
a wild blue bird under my heart.

Tonight I will be inconsolable.
Tomorrow I will refuse

to help you build again
the lie of *sanctuary*.

2.

Because I did not do it,
because I did not actually go,
I ride each night now in my dreams
over those long silver rails,
a driven engine, chugging and huffing.

But all the trains arrive in Waco
on the 52nd day:
buildings burning, children dead,
and a great wind raging off into the gulf
between *what is* and *what was possible*.

3.

Three stone angels guard them now, these children
who fell out of their lives and into these graves.

And where were they then, these angels
with faces that so resemble our own?

The Ones Who Come

1.

In Europe the books have opened again
to the pages of *terror* and *hunger*
as well as to all
the intricate names
of the lash and the whip.

The day and its disasters are singing
furiously in the faces of children.

You have told me your nightmares:
but the whole plain of Meggido
does not terrify me
as much as those children do
hung in their hunger.

Can you tell me how to go back to the daily
ceremony of my comfort and the abundant breaking of bread?

Whether or not we know how it happens,
out of each night's oblivion,
the next morning swims in.
And the next.
Likewise these children.

The last angels on earth have forsaken them:
in the steeple of time they are tolling like a bell.

2.

This angel has no wings.
This angel rises again
from the dust of the fields,
from the last bead of sweat and the oven's ash,
from the stench of cattle cars.
This angel takes the train
from Crakow every morning.
This angel travels with a sickle heart
and a yellow star to steer by.
This angel looks at you and that owl, Fear, flies through,
the heart crying, *who? who?*
This angel speaks and voices
rustle again in the meadow of birches:
here we are; here.

3.

They were children here so long. And now
their feet, their eyes, their little bones, their tongues
have fallen into the deep earth sleep. But tonight
their voices rise again through the winter thickets,
over the tiny white crosses and the bleak fields.

Look, I tell them, *I am trying*
to live my own life while I can.
Go back to sleep.

But there's no impressing them.
They go on tugging at their coatsleeves,
sucking on their fingers, go on crying, go on
holding out their invisible hearts, trying
to make themselves visible and loved again.

My heart barely endures it; but the moon,
oh the moon, she cracks easily. She is so far gone
tonight only the barest light remains to step out by,

and just as I think I've found a way
away from them, from the cries,
broken cups, frayed hems, I find instead that
they have somehow gathered themselves,
one by one, into my transient arms.

4.

With weeping, they shall all come home again.
—*Jeremiah 31*

Under the tongue, God's name
rests like a stone. Loose it
the wild lanterns of time
swing back, then forward.
I find myself in the ruins
of a house long ago blown down.
In my eyes, the dead
rise again and pass like light
over broken chimney brick.
They lie down on worn floorboards.
They cry all night with the pigeons.

5.

Children of holocausts, you come to me
over the dark currents of history.
I don't know what to do.
My own children rise up to me
wearing torn gowns, coats devoid of buttons.

Is the shape of the space I've eased into yours?

I too grow intimate with the earth,
all brambles and bright berries, clambering for sun.
No, not like that; not edible or sweet.
More like wild roses and thorns,
a barbed kiss left on the flesh
of those who have dared to touch me.

Fist over fist, the moon
still hauls itself across the sky
while Time's hand, like a godly woman,
takes me up and scours me clean.

I am thin as memory now.
But where you walk through
the trumpets of the body sound
and even the silent places in me shudder.

6.

No more lying awake until the animals
have sated themselves and the stars have gone out.
I want to sleep tonight.

I want to sleep though fields are burning
and the smell of ash is everywhere.
The wind is rising. The merciless snow is coming.
And what can one woman do against winter?

REFUGEE SCENES

Lines written while homeless

The season of snow arrives
with its old bitterness fastened on like buttons.

In the night: men arguing, boots
over broken glass and rubble,

an infant squalling for its mother,
and the last fires burning themselves out.

* * *

After the last fires burned out,
after the dead were loaded into wagons,
I followed your cart away into the woods
where you were to be left until morning.
I climbed up onto the wagon; I lay down next to you.
I held to you and waited all night for stars to come out
like a child again in a bed of darkness.

* * *

With cooking pots and sleeping children
on our backs, the iron lamp of the moon
not light enough for the roads again tonight,

nothing rushes to save us,
not even the last green shard of summer.

Why do we go on trying to push ourselves
through this darkness into the light again?

    *   *   *

Grief lights the way,
bright and stubborn as a moon.
And what would we have to promise
to sustain any heat we are offered tonight:
an apple bough? A bent limb? kindling sticks?
a red tricycle? a child? two?
the towns we have passed through on our way to this?
the deep forests of our own wooden hearts?

    *   *   *

I tell you, I would go willingly into exile
if I did not have to take my heart along.

Some nights now the dead
walk through me like a door.

When they do I pray.
Hard. All night.
On my knees like children do.

And what of the eyes of God?
Has someone also put them out?

In the Year of Our Lord

Christmas 1994

O small Lord of the manger, little
crèche of Christ where I have laid me
down to sleep like a dog at the master's feet
each time this year the stars have buckled
and darkness has fallen into me,

I cast my gifts before you now.

I give you back this night: *o holy night . . . good tidings . . .* all.
I give you peace on earth
as well as all the *thou shalt not*s
on which I cut my first teeth years ago;
also the shame I tucked beneath my pillow nightly as a child.

I have a penchant, a gift for sin

and there is no undoing it — only, always, You,
my redeemer of thorns and nails. Over the sleepy town
tonight the snow and cold prevail and the false
prophets of lights are loosed in every window
as far as I can see. Night falls. It falls, too, deeply into me.

But the jawbone of the ass is singing brightly

in my head, *Bring out your dead.*
And so I do.
I offer up the daughter, unnamed and blue,
unwrap the swaddling cloth, undo the ribbon, give her back.
Here, take the box she's laid in too.

The pietà we have made for years, the child and I.

Wait, there are more! (O see, I'm generous to a fault.)
Take also the children who, in this year of our Lord,
were dressed, hair combed, and laid to rest
in wooden boxes in the earth outside the hunger villages
while sweet milk curdled in our cups.

Over the earth tonight, that song.

And in the science closets somewhere,
quiet, other children sleep
curled 'round their fetal thumbs.
They've closed their eyes; they drift
now on the soured seas of formaldehyde.

O little crucifix, tell me what to do

with a tongue that goes on folding itself
around the shape of *Amen* year after year,
loss after loss, child after dying child? What do I do
in the year of weeping and wailing and gnashing of teeth,
my head thick with *Fear not, for behold,*

my soul howling, far off, leashed to the Word?

Each morning now, I sweep the dust and ash from this hearth,
send the soft, cast-off hair of the dog scurrying.
Voice of the whirlwind of my making, this:
sound of a broom over wooden floors,
sound like the hem of God's robe

moving through my house.

I, of the Storm

For a faith-healer friend, dying of cancer,
who has refused treatment

I, of the storm that your dying is,
    I, of the body's hungers and betrayals,
I, of the terror that walks by night
    and the seven last plagues of man,
                    I, of a too-small faith,
cannot mount the feathered
    backs of prayers and fly you off to safety.
Nor can I free myself of the deep
    winter of my own nature:
                    I want you to live.
But the river of your righteousness
    carries you off, a swift current running
down to God, and you do not look back.
    You leave me to my own devices
              which is why
I am fashioning for you a sea-worthy vessel.
    When the time is right, I will forge also
a dove, a bright olive branch,
    the moist tip of Ararat.

This Morning, Alice, Your Boots

Last night, you made your way to my table again
in spite of the early snow, a new bruise
running along your lower jaw and chin.
You're hiding them now: smudges of blue
and lilac, those almost-shadows shifting these days
over the stark planes and angles of your face. I noticed, too,
the bright stains you left like lipstick on the cup rim.

And when you noticed me noticing them
you blurted, *I'll leave him next time*
he touches me. You'll see.
But my kitchen, Lord, my kitchen
has rung with that promise for years.

I watched you storm away through the drifting snow
from my back door to yours and, as I watched you go,
I listened for the cries of late geese.
Four years ago, an early freeze like this fastened
five of them to the water's icy edge.
I stumbled on them at sunrise
while I was fouling a poacher's traps.

I thought I could help them get free, but every time
I came near, they pecked at me in terror
the way trapped things sometimes do
when they cannot distinguish between
what will save them and what will do them in.

Uphill again for half a mile, the dog and I,
for something to chop the ice away.
While I rummaged in the dank shed,
I could hear them complaining out on the pond.
Then downhill again with the axe
through the cold wind and trees.
But they had flown!

No, I *thought* they had flown.
Up close, I could see the ten stubbly sticks
of their legs still upright in the ice.
And, in the scuffed snow,
the poacher's tracks.

This morning, Alice, your boots:
one tipped drunkenly against the other
in your front hallway and the undertaker
making his way in through the snow,
past police lines and flashbulbs
and your husband's stunned, hung over
face framed in the cruiser's window.

EYE FOR AN EYE

If I could hate her like they do,
if I could hate her that much, I could want
her dead too, the anger which rises from hatred
rising like a fist, Alpha and Omega, omnipotent,
and maybe then I could forget, in such hard anger as that,
the two drowned boys as I imagine they must have been
that day, sleeping, strapped into car seats while she stood
in the Carolina sun, something snapping in her,
and sent the car over into the lake;

like that night when something snapped open in me
and, before it snapped shut again, I'd slammed
Earlie Jones' father so hard in the face
it broke his nose, so hard that his head
knocked back and cracked the wallboard behind
and he slid to the floor. The crowd in the E.R. cheered
when he went down; he hid
his face in his hands and sobbed.

When the doctor came out to tell him then
his boy had gone unconscious in the next room and died,
the drunk man's face went slack with what he'd done.
No one offered him anything then:
not a cloth for his nose, not a word.
So I slid down beside the man and held to him
until he held back to me and we wept and rocked,
like the world must have rocked under her that day
when she saw what she had done.

RED

In memory of the grandmother whose name I adopted

This bulging seam of blue between the thunderheads today:
the color of her eyes? No, but close enough after a storm
to make me think again of her.

Or maybe it's the red log cabin quilt I'm piecing:
nine reds ravishing the eyes like the reds
she painted her fingernails. How I envied
those long bright nails, that color,
I who, more than anything, wanted a red dress.

You had to notice her hands with color that bold
drawing the eye, and so you noticed too
the stub of the tenth finger and its neat white seam.
What made me ask again, that morning,
for the story of her finger? I'd heard it
many times by then; surely I had it by heart.

A brief bird, Memory, but it fluttered
in her eyes, those marble-blue eyes, as she told.
Everything too, not the story she spun for the rude
strangers who asked, the same story I'd heard for years
about her severing it in an airplane factory during the war.
I listened too, to every word, and never flinched, not once,

not the way my father flinched and winced last summer
when he told me that once she'd prostituted herself.
A hard word: *prostituted*. Different in the mouth
than "worked" or "labored."
A red word. Garish.
His tongue got hung on it.

I waited. But not one word from him
about his father who'd found her that night
in the kitchen, who'd made her confess what she'd done
then brought the hot knife down and maimed her.
Not one word about that
red, garish sin.

She told me that while she bled and tried to stitch
the bloody end closed with sewing thread,
he stood between her and the door.
Next time, he said, *I'll cut your face.*

How do I name this quilt, Grandmother, the bold red
pieces calling you back to me this morning?
Do I call it by your name, or mine?

Lizard Whiskey: A Parting Gift from Viet Nam

For Wayne Karlin

After the meal is done, your son draws it out
of the cool space under the kitchen counter.
When the jar is lifted free of the darkness,
the whiskey's tincture swarms with scales and flakes of skin
like a glittery storm in one of those Christmas snowglobes.

The lizard's been in there for years, gutted, giant,
doubled over himself in the quart-sized mason jar,
a smile on his wizened face, his eyes
almost rotted away; he is giving himself over
to the swirling and the darkness he's become a part of.

When the jar is tipped, a little of the whiskey
leaks onto the boy's hand, the stench of it
so foul we draw back from him as we once drew back
from ourselves in the long years of that war.
He wants to draw back too, but his hands
cradle the jar, the captive creature there,
and he does not let go his hold of it until he rights it finally
in a way that we haven't quite righted anything.

I look from his hands then to yours—thin, long-fingered,
elegant almost as a woman's—and I have to remind myself:
hands that turned a machine gun over a green country.
I look also at my hands which held the wounded of that time
and let some of them go, though I cannot say that
they have loosed their hold on me . . .

101

What kept him intact so long, this creature:
the darkness?—the fetid waters around him?
And what keeps us, despite ourselves, two creatures
curled and fetal inside that long-done war,
words falling from us like a storm?

THE MAN WHO STAYS SANE

St. Benedict's Asylum for the Mentally Ill, 1993

The man who stays sane in this world
    is doing a difficult work and you should

not trouble him with personal questions.
    Rather, ask him, "What do you think of Sarajevo?"

Or, "Who do you think will be president?"
    Or, "Do you think we will have peace in the Mideast?"

If you make small talk about the weather,
    he will tell you how reliable the sun is,

even after terrible storms.
    If you show him dark cracks in the sidewalk,

he will tell you it is from such places
    marigolds rise. Point out the rumpled man

sleeping on a bench next to him,
    he will tell you it's a good cloth for casual wear.

Ask him for money, if you must;
    ask what's in his pockets, but do not

ask his name, or the name of the town
    where he grew up. Do not ask him

if he ever loved a woman or had a son.
    His eyes are a window now on a blue-black sea.

Crimean. Sea dark as a bruise.
    He has dreamed lately

of going there to live again,
    has worked many years to acquire the fee.

If you do ask him, say, about his mother,
    he will tell you about her long dark hair

or her soft eyes, or that she sang to him;
    he will tell you he loved her.

He will fall silent then for a long time.
    You will have to wait, all morning maybe,

before he can tell you how, as a boy,
    he stumbled on her one morning and saw

the violence in her hands as she wrung and wrung,
    in the cold basin, the necks of his dead father's shirts.

Maybe he will tell you then how she hung them
    in the noonday sun to dry,

how she starched and ironed them, every one,
    how, when she came to the blue shirt

his father had loved best, she buried her face in it and wept,
    how she folded even that one finally and gave it,

with all his other belongings, to charity.
    If he only has one story now to tell,

let it be the one he loves.
    Let him tell it to you over and over.

Sit very still when he tells it, so still
    you can almost see the window on that sea

when it opens again and lets him in.

SUNDAY BRUNCH AT *THE OLD COUNTRY BUFFET*

Madison, Wisconsin, 1996

Here is a genial congregation,
well fed and rosy with health and appetite,
robust children in tow. They have come
and all the generations of them, to be fed,
their old ones too who are eligible now
for a small discount, having lived to a ripe age.
Over the heaped and steaming plates, one by one,
heads bow, eyes close; the blessings are said.

Here there is good will; here peace
on earth, among the leafy greens, among the fruits
of the gardens of America's heartland. Here is abundance,
here is the promised
land of milk and honey, out of which
a flank of the fatted calf, thick still
on its socket and bone, rises like a benediction
over the loaves of bread and the little fishes, belly-up in
    butter.

PERENNIALS

For my father, after a dream

I.

Everything over our heads now, out of reach
　　and dangerous—planes, planets and satellites,
　　　　telescopes, God and the reckless angels—

but you insist on a walk in the yard
　　at dusk, loving what puts down roots in the earth:
　　　　daffodils, red tulips, white roses, lilies,

thistle along the stone wall. No matter to you that
　　any of these could be torn by even a casual wind,
　　　　or a hard rain, or the snuffling yellow dog who sniffs,

then lifts his leg and douses the tulips good
　　while you look on and laugh. "I'm like them," you say,
　　　　scratching the dog's broad rump, "I keep making

a comeback, year after year." *Sure, Pop,* I think to myself,
　　and the sickness takes you out each winter
　　　　for a walk in a bleaker garden.

II.

Next year you could be too ill, you could be
　　too weary to walk. We'll sit together then, I guess.
　　　　Side by side, quiet, in the falling dark.

Just like when I was little: you
    watching the world. Me,
        watching you.

III.

You want to linger in the evening cool.
    I leave you there. When I look back
        from the window, it seems you sit too still;

you lean heavily, crookedly, in your chair.
    I run back through the yard; I kneel in front of you,
        my fingers fluttering for your pulse.

You wake then like a sleepy boy,
    smiling and rubbing your eyes.
        You ask, "Is it time to go?"

IV.

Not yet. Not yet.

V.

In the dream, sometimes, you lose yourself;
    you wander away from the garden
        at dusk. I am calling out to you.

So are the tulips and the bright
    stalks of gladiola. Also the yellow dog.
        God is calling too, I think,

and loudest of all.

GARDENS

For Jody Mahoney

The others hours-gone and I
am left again midmorning to swept floors, to dishes
racked and drying, to the old hum and order of a house
and this day turning like the morning's laundry in a hot dryer.

Outside, the first green grasses
struggle with dandelions between the flagstones
and the long beds of mud and mulch lie empty still,
hand-tilled and turned for planting weeks ago.

Somewhere, this morning, on the far edge of the continent,
you are under the knife and the needle,
and I am here, years past
trying to save anyone, past even believing that I can.

Because it is the only answer I have
to the darkness that being mortal is—
to loving what is also mortal and being done in—
I spend the morning on my knees,

pushing dormant bulbs into the earth,
trying to go so deep that I'm deeper in
than the palpable ache of the day,
the fist of fear clenching and unclenching in me.

*   *   *

I remember again the man who bought a plot of land
that had been a battleground, how he went on planting it
for years, though only weeds came up, and bitter waters after
    rain.

*   *   *

By afternoon, sun spills through the back windows
and the English ivy and creepers turn in their ceramic pots,
swiveling to embrace, in a few hours' time, what has fallen
    over them.
The Wandering Jew, too, turns from the exile of its corner.

Under the iron's heat, the starchy-sweet
scent of my husband rises from his shirt, so strong
I have to put the iron down and press my face into the cloth,
give myself over to what both is and is not there.

Beyond me, on the back deck, the windowbox dahlia
blooms and a stray calico moves along the wood's weedy
    edge.
I take it in and in: the gardens, the woods,
the vacant beds, the sun and soil.

There is never too much,
never enough.